Okay Now, Breathe...

Keeping the Faith through Life's
Unexpected Turns and Challenges

STEPHANIE B. DAVIS

Good Success Publishing
Okay, Now Breathe...
© 2020 by Celeste Owens

Visit www.surrendershop.com

All rights reserved. No part of this publication may be reproduced, stored in a retrieval system, or transmitted in any form or by any means-electronic, mechanical, photocopy, recording, or any other- except for brief quotations in printed review, without the prior permission of the publisher.

Requests for information should be addressed to:
Good Success Publishing, P.O. Box 5072, Upper Marlboro, MD 20775

ISBN: 9780997833294

Library of Congress Control Number:

This book is printed on acid-free paper. All scripture quotations, unless otherwise indicated, are taken from the New King James Version. Copyright © 1982 by Thomas Nelson, Inc. Used by permission. All rights reserved.

Cover design: Alexey Zgola
Interior design: Alexey Zgola

Printed in the United States of America

Dedicated to the most loved of sons, Ethan Davis.

REMEMBERING FOR ETHAN

From Your Father:

These are some things I saw and greatly admired about your mother. She was firm in her love and faith in God. She didn't live to impress people, she was who she was. If she believed in something, she was ALL in.

From Your Grandmother:

Your mom was the "go to person" in the family. We could talk to her about anything! She was trustworthy, talented and very comical. She was a tremendous help to myself and Pop Pop. She so loved you and your dad. I miss her more than words can say. Although she was here only for a very short 42 years, she left a great impact.

Love you always Brandy, Ma

Love you always Ethan, Nana

CONTENTS

Introduction 9
Victory is Here 11
God Is in Control 13
Fight to Believe 17
Faith's Declarations 23
Victory is Yours 25
Think Big 27
Pray with Power 31
Reject Rejection 35
Stay Alert, Stay Vigilant 41
Embrace the Illogical 47
Let Go 51
The Power of Forgiveness 55
Are you Dependent? 61
Little Become Much 65
Fear No More 69
Who's Your First Love? 73

Search God 77
Hope Against Hope 79
God's Way is Free 83
Trust the Process 87
Stay the Course 91
Are You in the Fight? 95
Journey with God. 99
Standing on His Promises. 103
You Will Find Him if You Seek Him 107
Find Success in Your Obedience 111
You'll See if You Believe 115
Judge You're Not 117
Drawing Closer to God 121
Faith that Moves 125

INTRODUCTION

Stephanie B. Davis, aka Brandy, worked with me from the inception of Dr. Celeste Owens Ministries. In fact, she and her husband Frank were the first to sow into the ministry. She was a true blessing to me personally and to the ministry generally. Not only did she handle the daily administrative tasks, but she prayed with me and for me daily.

These blogs come from a place of true love for God and people. Stephanie loved God and she loved people. Period. I remember when I first asked her to start writing the blogs for the ministry, she was hesitant; she couldn't see what I saw, that she was a great writer. But as she wrote more of them, her confidence increased and she surrendered to God's will for her life.

Although the blogs didn't receive hundreds of likes or comments, she didn't care. She just wanted to share and encourage. Now, I like to think that she is smiling from heaven knowing that far more will read her work in death, than they did in life.

Stephanie would write on all types of topics: decorating, health and wellness, current affairs, etc. However, what we have included in this book are the blogs that were personal for her. She had real life challenges, and on occasion a crisis of faith, but she overcame by the word of her testimony. She wrote from a place of freedom and struggle, peace and anguish, and love and pain. Although she struggled with issues we all struggle with, she managed to overcome through faith in God and full surrender to Him.

We are pleased to announce that every penny earned from the sale of this book will go to her son Ethan, as an inheritance from his mother who died at the tender age of 42. Though gone, she will never be forgotten.

Our hope is that you will grow in your faith, no matter what you are facing, as you read these timeless, heartfelt blogs from our daughter, sister, wife, mom and friend.

Okay now breathe...

Celeste Owens

CEO, Dr. Celeste Owens Ministries
Author, *The 40-Day Surrender Fast*
Loving Sister

VICTORY IS HERE

"Let not your heart be troubled; you believe in God, believe also in Me" (John 14:1).

Can you feel it? The sound of victory!!!

God is in total control and He's about to get the victory, and all the world will see. He's about to make one of the greatest 'comebacks' the world has ever laid witness to.

For those of us who truly understand, God has never left, He has always been with us. But for those who thought He had disappeared or had fallen asleep; you are about to witness the greatest 'comeback' you've never seen coming.

The Global Surrender Fast was just the start of something bigger than any of us. God is turning the hearts of His people back to Him.

"If My people who are called by My name will humble themselves, and pray and seek My face, and turn from their wicked ways, then I will hear from heaven, and will forgive their sin and heal their land" (2 Chronicles 7:14).

He's readying the body of Christ not only for unification, but for His return. This election has opened my eyes to just how divided the body of Christ truly is. And we know "that a house divided against itself, cannot stand."

It's imperative that we turn our hearts back to God, and repent; for then will we be able to clearly see God's plan revealed.

"And we know that all things work together for good" (Romans 8:28a).

"We are with you Father, so be lifted higher!"

Hallelujah, Hallelujah We Are Waiting, Hallelujah!

Daily Scripture Reading

John 14:1
Let not your heart be troubled; you believe in God, believe also in Me

Romans 8:28
And we know that all things work together for good to those who love God, to those who are the called according to His purpose.

GOD IS IN CONTROL

God is in control all the time.

Here's the news for today. I'm thanking God that he has brought to light what was hidden in the dark, so that all of us who seek the Lord will be able to go to Him and ask for His forgiveness.

I was one of those people who was saying "what is going on," "how long will we have to endure this injustice," and "why God haven't you done anything about it."

I was angry, and upset.

I realized I was mad at God.

I cried and cried throughout the night thinking about my loved ones and those who were mourning for theirs.

As I'm crying the scripture from 2 Chronicles 7:14 came to mind. I continued to cry and ignored what was in my spirit.

"If my people, which are called by my name, shall humble themselves, and pray, and seek my face, and turn from their wicked ways; then will I hear from heaven, and will forgive their sin, and will heal their land" (2 Chronicles 7:14).

The next day I was talking to my husband and he brought up the same scripture in reference to all the senseless deaths that have taken place in the last few days.

I immediately realized that this is not a woe is us thing; this is God bringing to light the workings of the enemy so we can turn to Him and pray.

He's allowing us to do something about it. His word says, "Call to Me, and I will answer you, and show you great and mighty things, which you do not know" (Jeremiah 33:3).

He's saying that we don't have to be in shock, without hope, or upset. All we have to do is turn to Him and He'll reveal to us what to do in times of trouble and distress. He'll prepare us. He'll give us wisdom, knowledge and understanding. He'll show us what to do. But we have to seek Him. We can't do what we think is best but we have to do what He knows is best.

Remember, we are in this world, but not of it. We are His people and He is our God. We have to follow His instruction.

This may appear to be a natural battle about race; but open your eyes because it's really a spiritual battle about power and the appearance that the enemy wants to display that we are without hope and that he's in charge. Matthew 24:24b says that if possible, through the workings of the enemy the very elect could be deceived.

But we know the truth!

The truth is, the enemy always comes LIKE!!! He's 'like' a mirage trying to appear as something greater than he is. He is without hope. He is doomed.

But if God shows us something, it's for our good. He shows us so that we can turn to Him for the answer.

He has the answer; will you listen?

Daily Scripture Reading

2 Chronicles 7:14
If my people, which are called by my name, shall humble themselves, and pray, and seek my face, and turn from

their wicked ways; then will I hear from heaven, and will forgive their sin, and will heal their land.

Jeremiah 33:3
Call to Me, and I will answer you, and show you great and mighty things, which you do not know.

FIGHT TO BELIEVE

"For I know the plans I have for you," declares the Lord, "plans to prosper you and not to harm you, plans to give you hope and a future" (Jeremiah 29:11).

This week I've come to the conclusion that I'm on the road to recovery. Recovery from what you ask?

Discouragement, disbelief, and hopelessness. In other words, a lack of faith.

This is unusual as it seems I was born for faith. Ever since I could remember I was believing for something.

I would believe for the smallest things like a trip to an amusement park, even though my mother already informed me we didn't have the money to go. To the biggest things like winning the Publishers Clearing House Sweepstakes which was worth 15 million dollars at the time. Well, the latter didn't come to pass, but you still couldn't convince me that my faith was useless. I still believed God could do the impossible.

"Now Faith is confidence in what we hope for and assurance about what we do not see" (Hebrews 11:1).

Fast forward to the present day. I now feel like a shell of my former faith-believing self.

I asked myself: *What went wrong? Where did I go wrong?* It didn't take me long to get the answer.

Several years ago, I was believing for the restoration of my brother's marriage. Me, alongside a couple of my sisters and my brother knew without a shadow of a doubt that restoration would happen. You could not have convinced us otherwise. We weren't just believing to believe, but we thought all signs were pointing towards restoration and that fueled our faith.

I tell you, we believed God so, that we thought we knew down to the day when it was to happen. So on that day that she was to return, we all came together by phone for prayer. At the end of that call we told my brother that we would talk to him *and* her later. We planned to celebrate.

It was after midnight and we hadn't heard back from him, but we just thought that he was probably too excited to call and we'd just talk to him a little later. Well, that later came, but not with the news we'd expected. She hadn't come back that day. I was crushed. I couldn't believe that something I thought God Himself had confirmed would happen, hadn't happened.

For some reason I wasn't able to recover as quickly as I had in the past. I mean this literally took everything out of me. And here I am today struggling to believe God. I didn't realize I was struggling until this week when I discovered that my actions are not lining up with what I say I believe.

Whatever you believe about yourself on the inside is what you will manifest on the outside.

My husband and I are believing for several things, but what I failed to see is that even though I was saying I was believing, I truly wasn't. When he would ask me what I thought God was saying, I would say, "what do you feel He's saying." When he would ask me to pray at night, I would always pray that God would help my husband to make the right decisions. When my husband wanted me to go get up with him at 6 am every morning, I always overslept.

It all of a sudden dawned on me that I truly don't believe what I'm saying I believe. I had placed all of our dreams on my husband's back and I was hoping that his faith would be enough.

But no more! I'm now determined to get my faith back because the word says:

"But without faith it is impossible to please him: for he that cometh to God must believe that he is, and that he is a rewarder of them that diligently seek him" (Hebrews 11:6).

I know that my husband needs me and I know that I need him, and together we need God to receive what He has placed in our spirits to ask for.

I am now challenging myself to fight for the faith that I once held so deeply. I'm not exactly sure where this road will take me, but I'm sure it will be better than the one that I've been traveling on for a while now.

"To contend earnestly for the faith which was once for all delivered to the saints" (Jude 3).

Are you lacking in the area of faith? I then challenge you to fight, believe and dream again for the things that God has spoken over your life. He's going to do it!!!

Daily Scripture Reading

Jeremiah 29:11
For I know the plans I have for you, declares the Lord, plans to prosper you and not to harm you, plans to give you hope and a future.

Hebrews 11:1
Now Faith is confidence in what we hope for and assurance about what we do not see.

Hebrews 11:6
But without faith it is impossible to please him: for he that cometh to God must believe that he is, and that he is a rewarder of them that diligently seek him.

FAITH'S DECLARATIONS

Your faith can make things happen!

The other day I woke up and heard softly, "Your faith can make things happen."

And it immediately sparked something in me; because for a long time my faith has lain dormant.

It was due to one moment in my life where I was believing God to work a miracle, and because it didn't happen the way that I believed it should happen, my faith was thrown off balance.

To be frank it became nonexistent.

But today my faith has been restored! And all because I heard those six words "Your faith can make things happen."

What God has spoken to me, I am now speaking it back to you.

Your Faith Can Make Things Happen!

"CALL THOSE THINGS THAT BE NOT AS THOUGH THEY WERE" (ROMANS 4:17).

Father, I pray that you would silence the noise, that comes to steal, kill and destroy. I pray that you restore, renew and make whole the faith that has laid dormant for so long, to become alive, fresh, and new. I pray that you open the eyes of your people and show them as you showed the prophet that was with Elisha, that they who be with us are more than they that be with the enemy. So, if we put our faith in You, You will never make us ashamed. In Jesus name, Amen!

Daily Scripture Reading

Romans 4:17
As it is written, "I have made you a father of many nations" in the presence of Him whom he believed—God, who gives life to the dead and calls those things which do not exist as though they did.

VICTORY IS YOURS

YOU WIN!

Who will stand against the Lord, No One Can! No One Will!
Who Will stand against our King, No One Can! No One Will!
Victory belongs to Jesus!!! Victory belongs to Him!!!
"If God be for Us, then who can be against Us!"

We Win!
We Win!
We Win!

We've already Won!!!

Everything is a process, but in the end, "We Win."

Everything that the enemy tries to pound into your mind and everything that was allowed to enter into your subconscious is and was a lie.

Those things, (trials) come to make us stronger.
What the enemy meant for bad...
JESUS!!! has made it well.
He's made it New!!!

We're no longer bound by the untruth; because we now know who is the truth.
God is the only True and Living God.
His Word is true! His promises are true!
If He said it, then it shall come to pass.

Choose the truth. Choose the Word of God.
Choose God!!! Choose Today Whom You Will Serve, and Never Look Back!

Victory Belongs to You!!!

Daily Scripture Reading

Romans 8:31
What shall we say to these things? If God be for us, who can be against us?

Romans 8:37
Nay, in all these things we are more than conquerors through him that loved us.

THINK BIG

SEEING WHAT GOD SEES

This week I just had a thought that I wanted to share…

It's a new year!

And with this new year comes a deeper understanding of God's word.
A deeper understanding of His plan.
A deeper understanding of His vision.
For some it will be a full manifestation of that vision.
And for others His Glory will be revealed.

"For now we see in a mirror, dimly, but then face to face. Now I know in part, but then I shall know just as I also am known" (1 Corinthians 13:12).

What happened in the past was not a mistake.
It may have been hard for some, but it wasn't a mistake.
It wasn't wasted time.
God didn't miss the mark.
He knew exactly what was happening, and it was for your good.

It might not have looked, felt or even appeared good.
But it *was* Good.
It was God.
Everything that happened was just the set-up for your future.
He is setting the stage for His Glory to be revealed.
In order to sculpt his children, God sometimes has to cause us to become malleable through our disobedience and hardened hearts

"But He knows the way that I take; when He has tested me, I shall come forth as gold" (Job 23:10).

As I'm sitting in my room writing, my son is walking out the door singing, "Don't know how but He did it!"

God has placed in us big things. "Think Big!" That's what He is saying this year.
You don't have enough?
You don't know enough?
You don't know how that can be possible?
Every thought you have. He knows. Tell it to Him.
Let Him increase your faith and watch Him move.
He's not moved by the things of this world.
He's moved by your faith.
God wants to see *your* faith!

Not that hidden faith, but that faith that sees and speaks it even before it happens.
What is God saying to you?
See it - I dare you!
Speak it — I dare you!
Yes!!! That thing *right there* that seems impossible, See it!!! That's the thing He wants to manifest in your life!

"Then Jesus answered and said to them, "Most assuredly, I say to you, the Son can do nothing of Himself, but what He sees the Father do; for whatever He does, the Son also does in like manner" (John 5:19).

The only way you'll be able to speak it is if you can see it. And when you can see it, you'll not only be able to speak it, but you'll be able to do it.
Now I ask you, What does your "BIG Faith" look like?

Daily Scripture Reading

1 Corinthians 2:9
But as it is written: Eye has not seen, nor ear heard, Nor have entered into the heart of man The things which God has prepared for those who love Him.

PRAY WITH POWER

PRAY THE WORD

On Thursday's Surrender Morning Prayer (we were on Day 18 of the Global Surrender Fast) I shared several prayers that the Lord gave me that speak life into my situations and not death. So often our prayers are just complaints or us informing God. But if we pray the Word of God, we have the ability to change not just our situations, but leave a legacy of prayer that will never die!

Sample prayers by category:

Forgiveness — Lord I messed up. Please forgive me for _____. I am grateful that your Word says if I come to you asking for forgiveness that you are faithful and just to forgive my sins and cleanse me from all unrighteousness. And Lord, although I may feel powerless to not do that sin again, Your Word tells me that I can do all things through Christ that strengthens me. Also, that when I am tempted, I don't have to be overtaken because you have provided a way of escape. Thank you, God for forgiving me. Amen.

Finances — God my finances aren't what I think they should be but I know that you are greater than all that troubles me. Lord Your Word tells me that You own everything and that every animal of the forest is Yours, and the cattle on a thousand hills. You've promised me that if I am faithful with a little, You will trust me with more. Lord I have been faithful. Thank you for honoring Your word in my life. Lord, I know this prayer isn't frivolous because Your Word tells me that money answers everything. Thank you for providing me with my answer. Amen.

Healing — You are good and Your mercy endures forever. There is no failing of Your love. I was young and now I am old, yet I have not seen the righteous forsaken or his children begging bread. So, I will not fear. Your Word tells me that it is good that I had been afflicted so that I may learn Your ways. But even in my affliction I know You to be Jehovah Rapha. Your Word tells me if you listen carefully to the LORD my God and do what is right in Your eyes, if I pay attention to Your commands and keep all Your decrees, You will not bring on me any of the diseases You brought on the Egyptians, for You are the LORD, who heals me. Amen.

Timing — Lord Your timing is perfect and I don't mind waiting on You. In fact, I don't want anything before

Your timing. Your Word tells me that the blessings of the Lord makes me rich and adds no sorrow with it. So, I will wait on Your good blessing. The Word also tells me that they that wait on the Lord shall renew their strength, they shall mount up on wings as eagles. They shall walk and not grow weary, walk and not faint. That promise is for me too. Your strength is made perfect in my weakness. So rather than say "how long", I'll say not my will, but Your will be done. Amen

Children — Lord Your Word tells me that children are a blessing and a reward from You. Thank you for my good gift You have given me. Your Word also tells me that you know the plans you have for my children, plans to prosper them and not to harm them, plans to give them a hope and a future. My child's future is bright in You. I don't care what it looks like right now, I believe it's already getting better because Your Word further tells me nothing is impossible for You. Therefore, since you have known my child before he/she was in my womb, I trust you to take care of Your child. I pray that he/she will grow in the grace and knowledge of You and find Your word more precious than pure gold and sweeter than honey from the honey comb. Amen.

Daily Scripture Reading

1 John 1:9
If we confess our sins, He is faithful and just to forgive us *our* sins and to cleanse us from all unrighteousness.

Philippians 4:13
I can do all things through [a]Christ who strengthens me.

Exodus 15:26
And said, If you diligently heed the voice of the Lord your God and do what is right in His sight, give ear to His commandments and keep all His statutes, I will put none of the diseases on you which I have brought on the Egyptians. For I am the Lord who heals you.

Isaiah 40:31
But those who wait on the Lord
Shall renew their strength;
They shall mount up with wings like eagles,
They shall run and not be weary,
They shall walk and not faint.

REJECT REJECTION

God doesn't call the qualified, He qualifies the called.

I thought this write up would be a great article to compliment Dr. Celeste Owens' talk about rejection, so I retitled this "Reject Rejection." Enjoy!

I'm not exactly sure why God created me. Life hasn't seemed to be all that it's cracked up to be.
As far as I can remember, I had never been happy in life. I feel as if I was born into depression.
My parents were, and are happy people.
So why does it feel like I was born to be miserable?
I was treated badly when I was in grammar school.
I was talked about to the point that I became suicidal.

"The thief does not come except to steal, and to kill, and to destroy. I have come that they may have life, and that they may have it more abundantly" (John 10:10).

From that moment on I developed a kind of pattern.

"I don't like myself today." (KILL YOURSELF!)
"I'm Ugly." (KILL YOURSELF!)
"No one likes me." (KILL YOURSELF!)
"I'll never be anything." (KILL YOURSELF!)
"Who'll ever love me?" (KILL YOURSELF!)

The enemy has a way of trying to shove something in your face or down your throat. He's always screaming LIES!!!

He doesn't play fair and he certainly doesn't play with honest intent.

That's exactly how my life ran before I accepted Christ into my world and began to see things differently. I'm what, as Dr. Owens and I have coined ourselves; *a least of these*.

A *least of these* is a person that has come from an unlikely background, and often has been made to feel like they would never amount to much of anything that matters; but is now destined for GREATNESS!!!

Are you *a least of these*?
Do you feel that you got the short end of the stick in this thing we call life?
Were you treated with disdain, raped, molested, beat, locked up, abandoned, lacked love or anything else that has plagued you into believing that you'll never be great?

If yes, then you are in good company.
Because guess what?
Your humble beginnings, or in-betweens doesn't determine your END!!!

David was so looked over that even when Samuel came to anoint the next king, David's own father didn't even see fit to call him to the ceremony. Psst! David became king by the way (see 1 Samuel 16:13).

Because of God's hand on Joseph's life, his brothers hated him so much, that they actually plotted to kill him; but their last-minute plans were changed and they were convinced to sell him instead. His brothers probably assumed that Joseph had been killed along the way, but he ended up becoming second in command to Pharaoh (see Genesis 41:1-45).

Rahab was a known harlot at the time that she helped the spies escape Jericho.
Her name is now listed in the genealogy of Jesus (see Matthew 1:5-16) and she is also mentioned in the "Great Hall of Faith" (see Hebrews 11:31).

I could go on and on…
"GOD QUALIFIES THE UNQUALIFIED."
If you notice, in the Word He's not disturbed or hindered by your flawed background. He uses it to bring glory to Himself.

Unlike the world that's looking for a warped sense of perfection, that is comprised of deceit, God is looking for someone who knows that they are flawed, and is transparent enough to allow Him to use them in a way that will bring healing and deliverance to others. Don't count yourself out. God is not finished with you, He's making you (see Philippians 1:6).

He's not caught off guard by what you've been through.
He's not shaken or rattled.
He knows you.
He loves you.
He's pleased with you.
You and your flaws are perfect to Him and He wants to use you for His glory.

All you have to do is believe the TRUTH above the lies.

Daily Scripture Reading

John 10:10
The thief does not come except to steal, and to kill, and to destroy. I have come that they may have life, and that they may have it more abundantly.

I Samuel 16:13
Then Samuel took the horn of oil and anointed him in the midst of his brothers; and the Spirit of the Lord came upon David from that day forward. So Samuel arose and went to Ramah.

Hebrews 11:31
By faith the harlot Rahab did not perish with those who [a]did not believe, when she had received the spies with peace.

Philippians 1:6
Being confident of this very thing, that He who has begun a good work in you will complete *it* until the day of Jesus Christ.

STAY ALERT, STAY VIGILANT

"Be sober, be vigilant; because your adversary the devil walks about like a roaring lion, seeking whom he may devour. Resist him, steadfast in the faith, knowing that the same sufferings are experienced by your brotherhood in the world" (1 Peter 5:8-9).

We're Dying!!!

Chronic illnesses, strokes, heart attacks, you name it. And this is happening as early as our thirties.

Yes, food is not what it used to be, but I'm talking about something more sinister. I'm talking about that silent killer called STRESS! The one that's taking out not just the unrighteous, but God's people as well.

Well since nothing's new under the sun, let's look at the Israelites from the Bible. God wanted to be their ALL, the One that they came to for everything, but they wanted a king to judge over them (see I Samuel 8:4-9).

In the wilderness they were told to discard of the leftover manna, but some didn't listen and the very next day it had rotted (see Exodus 16:19:20).

When God instructed Moses to send out men to spy out the land, they came back with a report that their enemies were too strong for them to defeat (see Numbers 13:16-33). Because of their distrust, lack of faith, doubt, rebellion, and sometimes outright refusal to obey God, they forfeited their inheritance (except for Caleb and Joshua, the rest never saw the Promised Land) and opted for stress instead. They literally took stress with them to their graves. Ouch!

Fast forward to today. Some of us are doing the exact same things that the Israelites were doing centuries ago, tenfold. We have access to more, and we think we need more. We're taking on additional jobs, hours, working during our vacation time, losing sleep and depleting our health all to obtain these things that we may never get to enjoy due to stress and all of the things that come along with that one word.

We were not created for stress and worry.

The Word says...

"No one can serve two masters; for either he will hate the one and love the other, or else he will be loyal to the one and despise the other. You cannot serve God and mammon" (Matthew 6:24).

The scripture above compels you to decide what the main thing in your life will be? If you decide to pursue money, people, status or anything that stands in the way of serving God, then you will begin to despise God, His Word, the specific Word He has spoken over you, His Voice, His servants, and everything that He stands for. You will begin to hate the very mention of His name.

"Do not lay up for yourselves treasures on earth, where moth and rust destroy and where thieves break in and steal; but lay up for yourselves treasures in heaven, where neither moth nor rust destroys and where thieves do not break in and steal. For where your treasure is, there your heart will be also" (Matthew 6:19-21).

We were and are created for Our Creator, Our God and Our King (see Revelation 4:11). Anything that God has not called us to do is now outside of His will. We were not called to please man. We were not called to appease our emotions. We certainly were not called to conform to the world's way of thinking (see Galatians 1:10).

So what do we do now?

Well I think it's time that we stop what we're doing, take a deep breath, and reassess. How will you use the little time you have left on this earth to do what is truly important?
How will you live out the rest of your days stress free?

Daily Scripture Reading

Matthew 6:25-34
25 Therefore I say to you, do not worry about your life, what you will eat or what you will drink; nor about your body, what you will put on. Is not life more than food and the body more than clothing?
26 Look at the birds of the air, for they neither sow nor reap nor gather into barns; yet your heavenly Father feeds them. Are you not of more value than they?
27 Which of you by worrying can add one cubit to his stature?
28 So why do you worry about clothing? Consider the lilies of the field, how they grow: they neither toil nor spin;
29 and yet I say to you that even Solomon in all his glory was not arrayed like one of these.
30 Now if God so clothes the grass of the field, which

today is, and tomorrow is thrown into the oven, will He not much more clothe you, O you of little faith?
31 "Therefore do not worry, saying, 'What shall we eat?' or 'What shall we drink?' or 'What shall we wear?'
32 For after all these things the Gentiles seek. For your heavenly Father knows that you need all these things.
33 But seek first the kingdom of God and His righteousness, and all these things shall be added to you.
34 Therefore do not worry about tomorrow, for tomorrow will worry about its own things. Sufficient for the day is its own trouble.

Revelation 4:11
You are worthy, O Lord,
To receive glory and honor and power;
For You created all things,
And by Your will they exist and were created.

Galatians 1:10
For do I now persuade men, or God? Or do I seek to please men? For if I still pleased men, I would not be a bondservant of Christ.

EMBRACE THE ILLOGICAL

Logical:

- Characterized by or capable of clear, sound reasoning.
- (of an action, development, decision, etc.) natural or sensible given the circumstances.

From the moment we're born we are taught to think logically. Growing up I'm sure you've said or mentioned something to someone that may have sounded a little out of the norm, only to hear, "Does that make any sense to you?"

On the flip side we've also learned how to throw logic out the window. Remember that thing that allows a car to fly, houses to be made out of gingerbread, fountains to be made out of Kool-Aid, and horses to be beautiful unicorns?

What's that thing called again? Oh yeah, imagination.

Imagination, also called the faculty of imagining, is the ability to form new images and sensations in the mind that are not perceived through senses such as sight, hearing, and other senses.

As kids we only needed to use our imagination to take us anywhere, we wanted to go or to be anything we wanted to be. And just like that it was because we created it.

The Word of God says speak those things that are not, as though they were. Speak it into existence (see Romans 4:17). If our imaginations could take us wherever we wanted and we could become whatever we wanted in our minds; imagine if we thought outside the box and refused to let logic stand in our way. What then could we accomplish? If we take a look inside our handbook (The Bible), we'll see that logic was never used to accomplish the works of God.

- David defeats Goliath (1 Samuel 17:1-58)
- Elijah, the widow with the handful of flour (1 Kings 17:7-16)
- Elisha, the widow with the two sons (2 Kings 4:1-38)
- King Jehoshaphat defeats the army's through prayer, fasting and praise (2 Chronicles 20:1-29)
- Peter walks on water (Matthew 14:22-33)

If you delve into a few of the stories above you will clearly be able to see that when it comes to faith and trusting in God's word, logic has no place in the outcome produced.

I, for one, am believing alongside my husband for the promises of God. The promises that He has revealed to us are so big that when I say we don't qualify for any of these miracles, believe me I'm not exaggerating one bit.

We've tried to be logical about this. I mean we've looked at it from every angle only to be disappointed. Then we were reminded that what God was going to do in our lives would not be able to be logically achieved. If they could be, we may or someone else may be able to take the credit for what only God could do. Let me just be the first to say that my family has decided to grasp and cling to the illogical.

I am still confident I will see the goodness of the Lord in the land of the living. Wait for the Lord. Be Strong + Take Heart + Wait on the Lord" (see Psalm 27-13-14).

Are you believing for something far beyond reasoning?

If the answer is yes, then what you must do is let go of everything you believed to be true (logical) and embrace what the world would call the irrational, unjustifiable and unsound reasoning known as faith.

Simply put trust beyond what you can see, hear and feel.

Daily Scripture Reading

Romans 4:17
(As it is written, "I have made you a father of many nations") in the presence of Him whom he believed—God, who gives life to the dead and calls those things which do not exist as though they did.

Psalm 27:13-14
13 I would have lost heart, unless I had believed
That I would see the goodness of the Lord
In the land of the living.
14 Wait on the Lord;
Be of good courage,
And He shall strengthen your heart;
Wait, I say, on the Lord!

LET GO

"Surrender to what is. Let go of what was. Have faith in what will be." Sonia Ricotti

All these years I've believed that if I wanted something to happen, I basically had to fill in some of the gaps to see it all come together.

If I couldn't do it then I'd find someone who could be of assistance.
If I didn't have the money at the moment, I would borrow.
If I couldn't do anything about it, then I guess that just meant it wasn't in God's will. (Well how about that?)

I have made a momentous discovery. If I just let God have full control, He'll work in a way I've never imagined could be possible.

That is what the Scriptures mean when it says, *"Eye has not seen, nor ear heard, nor have entered into the heart of man the things which God has prepared for those who love Him"* (1 Corinthians 2:9).

It's truly amazing what can happen when you decide to take the back seat and allow God to drive; you'll discover some pretty incredible things. First, you'll discover that God really has your best interest in mind. He doesn't just sit back and wait to see what you'll do, but He does wait until you come to Him.

"Call to Me, and I will answer you, and show you great and mighty things, which you do not know" (Jeremiah 33:3).

He loves each and every one of us so much and He desires to show us His strength in a great and mighty way. He wants to do big things in our lives. He wants to be big in our lives. He wants to be our God and He wants us to be His people.

The enemy has truly tried to pull the wool over our eyes. He has tried to make us believe that the God we serve is not loving, is not kind or giving. He has wanted us to think that God is overbearing and full of anger. But today I can truly say that's not the kind of God I serve. The God I serve wants the best for me. He wants to show me great and mighty things. He wants to lavish me with all kinds of wonders.

Thank you, Lord!!!

The hardest part of surrender is letting go, but once you do, you'll see that God is truly intentional concerning you. You'll discover just how into you He really is.

"Are not five sparrows sold for two copper coins? And not one of them is forgotten before God. But the very hairs of your head are all numbered. Do not fear therefore; you are of more value than many sparrows" (Luke 12:6-7).

The God we serve is worth both serving, and our surrender.

Have you surrendered today?

Daily Scripture Reading

1 Corinthians 2:9
Eye has not seen, nor ear heard, Nor have entered into the heart of man the things which God has prepared for those who love Him.

Jeremiah 33:3
Call to Me, and I will answer you, and show you great and mighty things, which you do not know.

THE POWER OF FORGIVENESS

Forgive, Forgiveness, Forgiven. Any way you look at it, it's not always easy to let go, give it, or receive it. There's something about that word that makes it difficult to understand. We may find ourselves giving "forgiveness advice" to someone, but then when that word reaches us and it's time for us to utilize it, it's not always the easiest thing to do. We understand the concept of forgiving, but executing forgiveness is a whole other thing in and of itself.

It just dawned on me a couple of days ago that I haven't forgiven someone of something that happened a while back. I kept saying within myself, "I don't care how they tried to make me feel or what their intentions were." I thought I had dismissed it; but what I realized was that I only masked it. I was pretending not to be bothered by what they said, when in reality their very thoughts of me were causing me to hate them. Notice I didn't say like, I said hate. It had gotten so bad and I hadn't even realized it.

I only had to face it when I was told that the person was going to be at an event that I was scheduled to attend. I instantly felt a rage inside of me. And that's when I had to confess to the Lord that I couldn't stand this person. I can truly say that once I could admit it first to myself, then confess it to the Lord, the rage was replaced with peace.

And now I'm on this journey called forgiveness.

I read this quote the other day, "I choose to forgive because it's more for me than for the person I am forgiving. It's my freedom from the sin of unforgiveness." (Unknown)

What is forgiveness?

- The act of forgiving someone or something.
- The attitude of someone who is willing to forgive other people.

Forgiveness is making a decisive decision to let go of the hurt caused by someone(s) or yourself; Letting go of the resentment you feel, and releasing it completely without thought of revenge or payback. When you forgive, you must acknowledge and not deny the hurt caused.
Denying that you were ever hurt or that you may have possibly hurt someone will only delay the process.

What are the physical benefits of forgiveness?

- Healthier relationships
- Healthier immune system
- Greater heart health
- Better self-esteem
- Decreased symptoms of depression
- Lower blood pressure
- Less anxiety, stress and anger
- Greater spiritual and psychological well-being

What are the spiritual benefits of forgiveness?

- A better relationship with God (Matthew 6:12-15)
- Able to empathize with others (*Matthew 7:3-5*)
- Greater Peace (Philippians 4:7)
- Able to reestablish relationships (Ephesians 4:32)

Why forgive?

I'm sure we've all heard that forgiveness is for us and by now it probably sounds so cliché'. But it truly is for us. God has given us several scriptures in the Word about forgiveness; and He does that so that we can see what not forgiving looks like.

We can't be one with the father if we don't forgive.
We can't be effective.
And we can't be forgiven.
It's not the easiest thing to do, but we have to do it.

How to Forgive?

Give it to God.
Find scriptures to help you through it.
Pray.
Trust God and believe He knows what's best.
Believe He can do what you can't do in your own strength.
God's patient, so He'll love you through this area if you'll only release it to Him.

"Forgiveness is not always easy. At times, it feels more painful than the wound we suffered, to forgive the one that inflicted it. And yet there is no peace without forgiveness."

Daily Scripture Reading

Matthew 6:12-15
12 And forgive us our debts, as we forgive our debtors.
13 And do not lead us into temptation,
But deliver us from the evil one. For Yours is the kingdom and the power and the glory forever. Amen.
14 For if you forgive men their trespasses, your heavenly Father will also forgive you.
15 But if you do not forgive men their trespasses, neither will your Father forgive your trespasses.

Matthew 7:3-5
3 And why do you look at the speck in your brother's eye, but do not consider the plank in your own eye?
4 Or how can you say to your brother, 'Let me remove the speck from your eye'; and look, a plank is in your own eye?
5 Hypocrite! First remove the plank from your own eye, and then you will see clearly to remove the speck from your brother's eye.

Philippians 4:7
And the peace of God, which surpasses all understanding, will guard your hearts and minds through Christ Jesus.

Ephesians 4:32

And be kind to one another, tenderhearted, forgiving one another, even as God in Christ forgave you.

ARE YOU DEPENDENT?

"Our dependence upon God ought to be so entire and absolute that we should never think it necessary, in any kind of distress, to have recourse to human consolations." Thomas A. Kempis

Something spiritually amazing happens when you let go of the reigns of dependence on people and become totally dependent upon God. His Anointing will rest on you and His Glory will be revealed. The place where you allow you and God to become one is called the road less traveled. The Word of God calls it the narrow road.

"Because narrow is the gate and difficult is the way which leads to life, and there are few who find it" (Matthew 7:14).

See we were born into this world system. We learned everything we needed to know about survival and how to succeed through the eyes of the world. We've become so dependent on the world's views and its road(s) to success that we rarely, if ever, even glance at that little narrow road.

"Enter by the narrow gate; for wide is the gate and broad is the way that leads to destruction, and there are many who go in by it" (Matthew 7:13).

Jesus said to Nicodemus, *"Jesus answered and said to him, "Most assuredly, I say to you, unless one is born again, he cannot see the kingdom of God"* (John 3:3).

That is Christ's commandment to us all. If we do not turn to Him then we will have no part with Him. Let's take that a step further. If we don't fight this flesh to renew our minds then we will not be able to discern the will of God for our lives and we will not be able to complete our assigned purpose on this earth.

"And do not be conformed to this world, but be transformed by the renewing of your mind, that you may prove what is that good and acceptable and perfect will of God" (Romans 12:2).

God has mapped out a plan for each and every one of us, and it probably will not look like the plan that He has for our neighbor. It's up to each of us to find out what God is saying and not depend on man to tell us God's plan. God is doing a new thing, and if you're not careful or you decide to follow someone else's road map, you may miss it.

Following someone else's road map or even your own fleshly-driven instincts (because instincts can be deceitful), will keep you on the wide path; but depending totally on God and His word for your life will put you on the road that is often consciously or unconsciously avoided.

"That's not the way it's ever been done."

"We've never done it like that."

"You can't do it that way."

"There are steps you have to take and you won't make it if you don't take them."

That's the advice you may get from men if you choose to follow their ways.

God said He's doing a sudden thing, which means that all the steps that others had to take, you'll avoid because of your total dependence on God in this season. You will effectively bypass the long circuitous route that may lead to an unsatisfying end that doesn't yield fruit.

Your dependence will take you from here to there, all because you are doing, just as His Son, only what He sees the Father doing (John 5:19).

That's dependency!!!

"Jesus said to him, "I am the way, the truth, and the life. No one comes to the Father except through Me" (John 14:6).

Total dependence is the only way you will succeed!

Daily Scripture Reading

Romans 12:2
And do not be conformed to this world, but be transformed by the renewing of your mind, that you may prove what is that good and acceptable and perfect will of God.

John 5:19
Then Jesus answered and said to them, "Most assuredly, I say to you, the Son can do nothing of Himself, but what He sees the Father do; for whatever He does, the Son also does in like manner.

John 14:6
Jesus said to him, "I am the way, the truth, and the life. No one comes to the Father except through Me.

LITTLE BECOME MUCH

"When the day was now far spent, His disciples came to Him and said, "This is a deserted place, and already the hour is late. Send them away, that they may go into the surrounding country and villages and buy themselves bread; for they have nothing to eat." But He answered and said to them, "You give them something to eat." And they said to Him, "Shall we go and buy two hundred denarii worth of bread and give them something to eat?" (Mark 6:35-37).

Have you ever thought, *what do I have to offer? I'm not good enough, smart enough, pretty enough, athletic enough, and so on and so forth*? I mean the flesh will always be able to come up with something to make you feel like nothing; to stop you dead in your tracks. There will always be a "not enough" in your life that will try to hinder or completely stop you from fulfilling your destiny.

When it dawned on the disciples that the people had to be hungry from sitting and listening to Jesus the whole day, they came to Jesus and said, "Send the people away so that they can go buy food and eat." But Jesus said to the disciples, "You feed them." They were obviously not expecting that response, as they replied "with what? We'd have to work months to earn enough money to buy food for all these people!" You could tell by the response that the disciples probably felt overwhelmed.

When we're overwhelmed by something the first thing that usually appears is fear followed by anger. Fear may result because we don't feel at all qualified, and anger because we can't believe that we would be asked to do something we don't feel adequate enough to do. But the Word of God says,

"I can do all things through Christ who strengthens me" (Philippians 4:13).

So in essence what He was saying to the disciples when He said "you feed them" was that although they didn't know it, they had more than they realized they had to sustain the crowd. In their obedience they presented two fish and five loaves of bread. Jesus took what they had, and then He looked up to heaven, blessed and broke the loaves, and fed the multitude.

What He said to the disciples back then is what He's still saying to each and every one of us today: what He has placed inside of us from the beginning of our conception until the time of our natural death, is more than enough to accomplish that which He is calling us to. It may seem like you can't get the job done and that would be correct, you can't. But relying solely on God and allowing Him to infuse you with His power will bring out things in you that you've never imagined.

You are more than capable.

You have been equipped.

And you can do all things through Christ who strengthens you.

So, bring what you have, offer it to God and feed the multitude

Daily Scripture Reading

Mark 6:35-37

35 When the day was now far spent, His disciples came to Him and said, "This is a deserted place, and already the hour is late.

36 Send them away, that they may go into the surrounding country and villages and buy themselves bread; for they have nothing to eat."

37 But He answered and said to them, "You give them something to eat." And they said to Him, "Shall we go and buy two hundred denarii worth of bread and give them something to eat?"

Philippians 4:13
I can do all things through Christ who strengthens me.

FEAR NO MORE

Everything you want is on the other side of fear.

Terror, Fright, Horror, Alarm, Nervousness, Unease, and the list goes on and on. These are all words that describe FEAR!

Fear: An unpleasant emotion caused by the belief that someone or something is dangerous, likely to cause pain, or a threat.

I wrote about my experience with fear awhile back, and I've come to realize that fear is a journey. Even after you decide to face it, you become overtly aware that fear has a lot of tricks up its sleeve. I've come to realize that fear is the silent and deadly killer to dreams and aspirations. It's so quiet that you're not even aware that it has attacked or attached itself to you until it's exposed. Whew!!! That means you can be walking around with fear right now and not realize it. It's so conniving that it'll make you believe that you don't want to do something that you've always desired to do.

The opportunity will present itself and because you don't realize that fear is controlling you, you'll pass up the opportunity and not even understand why you did that. Or you may be one who knows that you are fearful and still chooses to pass up opportunities out of fear. You may have decided that fear is what it is and it's here to stay, so you might as well get used to it. Pssst! Fear is not real, it's a fleshly emotion and like any emotion, we can choose to accept it or reject it.

Fear – forget everything and run or face everything and rise. It's your choice.

I must admit that fear is a passive aggressive emotion. It wants to do either nothing or it wants to do it in a way that will surely not be pleasing to God or anyone else because it's selfish. Back fear up in a corner and it will most likely become defensive and agitated.

Fear doesn't think about anyone or anything else. It's just concerned about what will benefit it (fear). Which means that it can't and will never be beneficial to the Kingdom (Romans 8:7-8). Fear may seem like it's trying to protect you from something bad, but when fear shows itself at a time when it's most beneficial to you and others, especially God, then fear has chosen not to work for you, but against you. Because the word says...

"God is our refuge and strength" (Psalm 46:1).

God has given us a choice in everything. We can choose to live fearfully and defeated, or triumphantly and free. As Les Brown says, "will you choose to live your dreams or will you decide to be content living your fears?"

Daily Scripture Reading

Romans 8:7-8

7 Because the carnal mind is enmity against God; for it is not subject to the law of God, nor indeed can be.

8 So then, those who are in the flesh cannot please God.

Psalm 46:1

God is our refuge and strength,

A very present help in trouble.

WHO'S YOUR FIRST LOVE?

FIRST
LOVE
COMING BACK TO JESUS

Remember the song by Jonathan Butler, "Falling in love with Jesus?"

Remember the first day you accepted Jesus Christ into your life? Nothing else mattered! Church was now exciting, People were beautiful, and Jesus was magnificent! The sun seemed brighter, the grass seemed greener and just like being transformed into a beautiful butterfly, life became a world of endless possibilities.

Now, fast forward a bit. You've experienced things or you've been through things you've never thought you'd have gone through. Life has knocked you around. Your nemesis (the devil) has tried to destroy you on quite a few occasions. And it appears that your vision has become a bit blurry. Church doesn't seem as bright as it used to. People look less engaging. And well, the appeal of Jesus has faded a tad bit. So I ask, where has your first love gone?

I know for me as I mentioned in an earlier blog, that the issue was faith and accepting that no matter how much faith I had about a certain thing or how much I believed it was going to happen, it not happening had nothing to do with me, but the will of God. I thought, if I would've done it this way or that way, then maybe there would have been a more favorable result.

If I would've believed harder.
If I would've fasted harder.
If I would've prayed harder
If I would've...

And still at the end of the day it just wasn't God's will. Do you feel that way? Well you are certainly not alone. See, one of the biggest tricks that the enemy tries to feed us is deception. He tries to make us believe that what we've been through is for us alone. But that most certainly is not the truth. And, even though you feel that a certain thing should've worked out a certain way. God wants to show you a better way.

Sometimes when things are falling apart, they may actually be falling into place.

And he also wants to show you your best life now. Now is not the time to get discouraged or down. And it's certainly not the time to distance yourself from the Lord. But now is the time to fight like never before. Because there is something that the devil is afraid that you and I might find out.

What the thief doesn't want you to know! (see Romans 8:37). It's time that our soul be reunited with its first love, and that we allow God to set us on fire once again.

Daily Scripture Reading

Romans 8:37
Yet in all these things we are more than conquerors through Him who loved us.

Romans 8:28
And we know that all things work together for good to those who love God, to those who are the called according to His purpose.

SEARCH GOD

Are you looking for direction? Do you feel lost? Do you feel hopeless? Do you feel like life is passing you by? Well then, the first and only thing you need to do is stop what you're doing, Pray, ask God for Direction and get into The Word.

"Trust in the Lord with all your heart, and lean not on your own understanding; In all your ways acknowledge Him, and He shall direct your paths" (Proverbs 3:5-6).

That's it! It's just that simple. Stress and depression are not required. Having a pity party or beating yourself down first is not a prerequisite for fulling your destiny. Trusting and taking God at His word is required. It doesn't matter where you start, because it's all about the finish. If God has called you, then you better believe that He has equipped you with everything you need to fulfill your assignment.

"Moreover whom He predestined, these He also called; whom He called, these He also justified; and whom He justified, these He also glorified" (Romans 8:30).

He will not reveal everything to you all at once, but as you continue to trust, lean and depend on Him, the picture will become clearer. Your perception of things will fade and God's truth will prevail.

For you are, The Head and Not the Tail,
You are Above only and Never Beneath,
You are the Lender, Never the Borrower,
You Can do all things through Christ who gives you strength,
Because you are His perfect divine creation and you're fearfully and wonderfully made.
Don't be fooled by our adversary. God is with You!!!

Daily Scripture Reading

Proverbs 3:5-6
5 Trust in the Lord with all your heart, and lean not on your own understanding; 6 In all your ways acknowledge Him, and He shall direct your paths.

Romans 8:30
Moreover whom He predestined, these He also called; whom He called, these He also justified; and whom He justified, these He also glorified.

HOPE AGAINST HOPE

Even when there was no reason for hope, Abraham kept hoping. He was fully convinced that God is able to do whatever He promises. (Romans 4:18, 21)

Faith is defined as a...

1. Complete trust or confidence in something or someone.
2. Strong belief in God or in the doctrines of a religion, based on spiritual apprehension rather than proof.

Have you ever had to, or are you trusting God for something that is so beyond belief that your psyche can't even comprehend? Now try telling someone else what God wants to do and watch the look of sheer bewilderment on their face. When you're believing God for something that is so big that it doesn't really make any sense, your flesh mind will immediately begin to fight against your spiritual mind with logical reasoning. It will tell you the truth of the situation and expect you to accept it. It doesn't understand faith-based belief.

"For to be carnally minded is death, but to be spiritually minded is life and peace" (Romans 8:6).

My husband and I are believing for something right now that is so big, that we know that we have to have faith and have it to ourselves. It's almost impossible in our faith walk at this time to explain what God wants to do for us. We've tried to explain it to some, but when you don't have a clear view of the vision that is to come to pass, it's hard to answer all the questions coming at you. Have you ever tried to explain what God is doing and then you yourself become confused? You're all of sudden sitting there like why should this happen for me? Who am I to believe so big? How in the world does this make any sense? Yikes!!! It doesn't make any sense!

FLESH vs. SPIRIT

Then you have to regroup and get back on track, and I mean quick, fast and in a hurry. Because time is definitely of the essence when your spirit is fighting against your flesh. Any amount of leeway you give to the flesh during this crucial time will determine the next step you make. The flesh is just waiting for an opportunity to get you off track. During this time, it's imperative that you become quiet, so that you can hear clearly from God. The enemy will be right on your back, so you have to be tuned in to the spirit. If you desire to share what you're believing God for, make sure you acknowledge the Holy Spirit and wait on his leading. It may at times be very beneficial for you to have someone else fighting for the blessings with you. Whatever you're believing God for, don't let go. Believe beyond what you can see. Trust in it no matter what the situation looks like and hold on for dear life. It may not be easy, but it will be worth it.

Daily Scripture Reading

Romans 4:18, 21
18 who, contrary to hope, in hope believed, so that he became the father of many nations, according to what was spoken, "So shall your descendants be."
21 and being fully convinced that what He had promised He was also able to perform.

Romans 8:6
For to be carnally minded is death, but to be spiritually minded is life and peace.

GOD'S WAY IS FREE

Stress is defined as: "A state of mental tension and worry caused by problems in your life, work, etc., something that causes strong feelings of worry and anxiety; physical force or pressure."

Just A Thought....

Today we're living in a fast-paced world. Everything is rapidly changing. We live in a time where it's in with the new and out with the old. And sometimes you may feel the pressure to keep up. And if you're not feeling the pressure, maybe you have kids who feel the pressure and therefore you now feel pressured. It's all about the latest shoes, clothes, tablets, iPads, cell phones, and whatever else floats our way. Things are moving so fast that we don't even get the chance to enjoy what we already have. It's easy to become ungrateful and stressed out about how to get our hands on the next big thing. So, what happens when we give in to those temptations?

We may pick up more hours on our jobs.
We may pick up a second or third job.
We may even decide to turn to credit cards (Yikes!).
We become stressed out, burned out, as well as physically and mentally drained. We get so caught up in the "I want the best and I want my family to have the best" that we miss out on the most important parts of life, specifically spending time with God, Family, Friends and Ourselves.

When was the last time you were just able to relax your mind long enough to not think about anything except what's right in front of you?

"Now acquaint yourself with Him, and be at peace; Thereby good will come to you" (Job 22:21).

Remember the saying that the best things in life are free? I'm starting to realize just how true that statement really is. Going to the park, taking a walk, watching a movie and praying together are things you can do with your loved ones. And it's free! Free I tell you! It allows you to not only get in valuable time you'll never get back, but it also allows you to become more tuned in to what's really important in life. It also allows you to draw closer to God, by drawing closer to the things that are important to him, mainly His people. Isn't it so good to be surrendering to Him right now? We not only get a chance to draw closer to our Creator, but we'll also get a chance to draw closer to the things of true importance because we're drawing closer to Him.

Daily Scripture Reading

Job 22:21

Now acquaint yourself with Him, and be at peace; Thereby good will come to you.

TRUST THE PROCESS

FEAR NOT!

The atmosphere is changing now, For the Spirit of the Lord is here. The evidence is all around, That the Spirit of the Lord is here. -Elevation Worship

"Fear not, for I am with you; Be not dismayed, for I am your God. I will strengthen you, Yes, I will help you, I will uphold you with My righteous right hand" (Isaiah 41:10).

God has a plan for your life, and it's unique and purposeful. So rest in it! You can trust it!

Even when you think that you're getting nowhere, and you want to throw in the towel; take a moment and BREATHE! Inhale the Spirit of God and exhale the spirits of doubt, anxiety, fear and dismay. BREATHE!!!

"So he answered, "Do not fear, for those who are with us are more than those who are with them" (2 King 6:16).

For the promises of God are bigger than your circumstances, your finances, your background, your past, present and future.

"For all the promises of God in Him are Yes, and in Him Amen, to the glory of God through us" (2 Corinthians 1:20).

God is saying, "Didn't I tell you that you would see My glory if you believe?" He wants to use you so that His glory may be revealed and so that others will believe! The journey will not always feel comfortable, or even worth it at times; but if you just make up in your mind to plant your feet on this good ground, you will in the end see that it was worth every tear you've ever had to release to get to this moment. In other words, yes it will have been well worth it. So trust the process. Stay focused and be relentless in pursuing the promises of God. He loves you! And even in moments when you feel all alone, just know that He said that He would never leave you, nor forsake you. He's here! Just reach for Him!

Daily Scripture Reading

2 King 6:16
So he answered, "Do not fear, for those who are with us are more than those who are with them."

2 Corinthians 1:20

For all the promises of God in Him are Yes, and in Him Amen, to the glory of God through us.

STAY THE COURSE

FEAR NOT FOR I AM WITH YOU, says the Lord.

God is with you! For all of you who God has called to the secret place, know that He is with you. This is the place where you find rest. Rest from all the demands of this world system. You'll find clarity and your mind will surely be renewed.

"He who dwells in the secret place of the Most High shall abide under the shadow of the Almighty" (Psalm 91:1).

You will become all that God has created you to be if you'll only rest in Him. You may be saying that ever since you entered into His rest it has been nothing but an upward battle. Well, let me be the first to say that the moment you said yes to God the fight officially began. The spiritual battle between heaven and hell just got real in your life. Know this, God will win but the enemy wants you to believe that you are in a no-win situation. He wants you to give up! But if you will just stay the course "YOU WILL SEE GOD AND HIS GLORY IN THE LAND OF THE LIVING!!!"

Don't give up. Fight for the promises of God. It's worth it. I'm fighting right now and I refuse to give up. He's worth it! I promise you He is. He wants to give you as much of Him as you can stand. If you allow Him to, He will show you that He can be everything you've ever imagined Him to be and then some. You will never want for anything if you will stick with and stay close to God. I *feel* that in my spirit. What God has planned for people who love Him is more than *eye has seen, or ear heard, nor has never even entered our minds.* (see 1 Corinthians 2:9).

You can't give up! You have to make a conscious decision that you will dig deep into the trenches and you will stay there until you see the manifestation of God's promises. They're coming. No matter how bleak it looks His promises are yes and amen. You win! You'll look back one day and you'll have the testimony that it wasn't always easy, but it was worth it. One day you'll say, just as I'm going to say, "I wouldn't have changed a thing." God is real! His promises are true and His word is above His name. If He said He'll do it, consider it done.

Daily Scripture Reading

Psalm 91:1
He who dwells in the secret place of the Most High shall abide under the shadow of the Almighty.

1 Corinthians 2:9
But as it is written: 'Eye has not seen, nor ear heard, nor have entered into the heart of man the things which God has prepared for those who love Him.

ARE YOU IN THE FIGHT?

You shouldn't give up. Fight for yourself and who you are. You've got to go through the worst times.

I think today is a great day to start back on the road to trusting God.

Sometimes the storm may get so hard that it seems like the only way to get any relief is by occupying your mind with something else. It's usually not even intentional. That reality TV show, that delicious sweet you can't seem to live without, shopping without purpose, internet surfing with no direction, or just becoming a couch potato and watching movie after movie. Anything to bring peace to your surroundings and current situation.

I've buried myself so far down in the rabbit hole that I couldn't see my way out. I mean God has taken my family and I to the unknown and it has been so overwhelming at times that before it even dawned on me what I was doing, I had started using YouTube makeup and natural hair tutorials as my escape. I had gotten so bad that even when my husband would come to me to discuss our situation, I would be like "whatever you want to do is fine." Seriously? I had totally checked out; not just on my family but on life in general. I totally stopped looking to God and I started getting caught up in how I felt. Why us? Why do we have to do this? Who are we to do something that doesn't make sense and believe that it will even work out?

At one point I got so upset that I decided I wasn't going to do anything until God explained it to me. Imagine putting God on a time frame to explain Himself. And because He didn't explain anything, I didn't want to hear anything related to our situation. I would become so irritated when someone would prophesy to us. I would go to church letting God know I didn't want to hear anything from anyone trying to say anything personal pertaining to our situation. And it never failed, someone would always say something. Can you relate? The struggle can seriously be real sometime guys.

Alistair Begg says, "There are times in our Christian life when we cannot see beyond the next step. At that point, we have to trust God and venture out on the basis of His Word."

Today I am encouraging you to get back in the fight. Don't get defeated; get up determined to beat that doubt, that disbelief and that 'why me?' mentality.

Are you ready to fight?

Daily Scripture Reading

Ephesians 6:10-18

10 Finally, my brethren, be strong in the Lord and in the power of His might.

11 Put on the whole armor of God, that you may be able to stand against the wiles of the devil.

12 For we do not wrestle against flesh and blood, but against principalities, against powers, against the rulers of the darkness of this age, against spiritual hosts of wickedness in the heavenly places.

13 Therefore take up the whole armor of God, that you may be able to withstand in the evil day, and having done all, to stand.

14 Stand therefore, having girded your waist with truth, having put on the breastplate of righteousness,

15 and having shod your feet with the preparation of the gospel of peace;

16 above all, taking the shield of faith with which you will be able to quench all the fiery darts of the wicked one.

17 And take the helmet of salvation, and the sword of the Spirit, which is the word of God;
18 praying always with all prayer and supplication in the Spirit, being watchful to this end with all perseverance and supplication for all the saints.

JOURNEY WITH GOD

I Need Thee, Oh, I Need Thee;
Every Hour I Need Thee;
Oh, Bless Me Now, My Savior,
I Come to Thee.

That song now rings fresh in my mind. It's a clear reminder from my soul that I should never forget what's most important as I take this journey on this narrow road.

Surrendering to God can sometimes be challenging because of the flesh. The flesh refuses to submit; thereby making it easy to feel the need to give up and simply surrender to self. But I know that if I just hold on, and resist the will of my flesh, then I'll be able to submit and become one with God's will. God has called us to a place in Him that would otherwise not be possible without our full submission.

Where He's taking us, we cannot achieve in our own might. WE NEED GOD!

What He's doing in us is truly the impossible and we have to totally rely on him and lose our logical thinking in order for His will to be manifested in our lives.

Now I'm sure it's not just me that He's offering a life without limits, restraints, walls, or borders. I'm sure he's calling some of you as well.

"For many are called, but few are chosen" (Matthew 22:14).

I can't emphasize enough the need to simply trust God. Stop looking at the outward man and look inward to the soul, where neither moth nor rust destroy. That's where you'll find God. That's where you'll find life, meaning and purpose for your life.

God has a plan for you that goes beyond understanding and reasoning. He just needs your cooperation to give you your best life now. Will you accept? You are invited.

Daily Scripture Reading

Matthew 22:14
For many are called, but few are chosen.

Zechariah 4:6

So he answered and said to me: This is the word of the Lord to Zerubbabel: 'Not by might nor by power, but by My Spirit,' Says the Lord of hosts.

STANDING ON HIS PROMISES

"But those who wait on the Lord shall renew their strength" (Isaiah 40:31).

Maybe you're waiting on, or in the process of waiting on God. How's it going? Are you feeling victorious or loss and apprehensive? Maybe a little in between? During this time of waiting it's imperative that you get into a place where you can be silent. Because it will take silence, perseverance, and determination to surrender your will to God's will.

God has revealed to you something He wants to do in your life and it may appear strange, out of the norm, or downright impossible to others. Your loved ones or friends may doubt that you have heard from God and appeal to your sense and reason to change your mind. Furthermore, your sharing may bring about jealousy, and some may just want to talk you out of it because they don't want to see you succeed.

Know that while you're waiting on God it may seem like nothing is happening. It may feel like time wasted, energy needlessly exerted and the question that you'll ask yourself time and time again…"Did I really hear from God?"

You are not alone. But there really are benefits to waiting and once you see those benefits, waiting won't be hard. It will get easier and easier. You'll see God at His most powerful during this time.

"And He said to me, 'My grace is sufficient for you, for My strength is made perfect in weakness.' Therefore most gladly I will rather boast in my infirmities, that the power of Christ may rest upon me" (2 Corinthians 12:9).

You'll become who you were intended to be from the beginning (see Jeremiah 29:11). We grow and mature while we wait.

"But He knows the way that I take; when He has tested me, I shall come forth as gold. My foot has held fast to His steps; I have kept His way and not turned aside" (Job 23:10-11).

As you can see, you're in the perfect hands of God. So rest and know that God is on your side.

Daily Scripture Reading

Isaiah 40:31
But those who wait on the Lord shall renew their strength; They shall mount up with wings like eagles, They shall run and not be weary, They shall walk and not faint.

2 Corinthians 12:9
And He said to me, "My grace is sufficient for you, for My strength is made perfect in weakness." Therefore most gladly I will rather boast in my infirmities, that the power of Christ may rest upon me.

Jeremiah 29:11
For I know the thoughts that I think toward you, says the Lord, thoughts of peace and not of evil, to give you a future and a hope.

Job 23:10-11
But He knows the way that I take; when He has tested me, I shall come forth as gold. My foot has held fast to His steps; I have kept His way and not turned aside.

YOU WILL FIND HIM IF YOU SEEK HIM

"Be diligent to present yourself approved to God, a worker who does not need to be ashamed, rightly dividing the word of truth" (2 Timothy 2:15).

Now is the time to seek the Lord. There are so many things going on in the world today; random terrorist attacks, senseless killings, suicides, job loss, depression, hearts being deceived and people becoming more and more desensitized to the needs and well-being of others. And why is that? I believe it's because we've become so overwhelmed with what we SEE and how we FEEL about what we see, that we've taken our focus off of God and the Word and have taken matters into our own hands. The result? Messed up lives. But now is the time to seek the Lord.

The benefits of seeking God through His word are endless: feelings of peace in a chaotic world, situations working out because you took your hand off of them, the ability to love your enemies and abstain from temptation. All these become second nature when you seek the Lord.

"Be anxious for nothing, but in everything by prayer and supplication, with thanksgiving, let your requests be made known to God; and the peace of God, which surpasses all understanding, will guard your hearts and minds through Christ Jesus" (Philippians 4:6-7).

Now is the time to seek the Lord. How do you maintain that peace? Simply by keeping your heart and mind stayed on the Lord and getting into your Word daily. Not just reading the Word, but actually meditating on it and getting revelation and understanding through the Word and how it relates to you.

"This Book of the Law shall not depart from your mouth, but you shall meditate in it day and night, that you may observe to do according to all that is written in it. For then you will make your way prosperous, and then you will have good success" (Joshua 1:8).

Now is the time to seek the Lord. The advantages of really studying the Word opens us up to endless possibilities. We begin to see things the way they truly are, and not the way they appear to be. We get closer to

God and then we are able to become our true authentic selves.

"And do not be conformed to this world, but be transformed by the renewing of your mind, that you may prove what is that good and acceptable and perfect will of God" (Romans 12:2).

If you're wanting to get into your Word and not exactly sure where to start, here are a few suggestions:

1. Acknowledge the Holy Spirit and let him speak to you.
2. Look at what's going on around you and pull a scripture that pertains to your situation and mediate on it.
3. Download a Bible app and start a reading plan that interests you.

Daily Scripture Reading

2 Timothy 2:15
Be diligent to present yourself approved to God, a worker who does not need to be ashamed, rightly dividing the word of truth.

Philippians 4:6-7
6 Be anxious for nothing, but in everything by prayer and supplication, with thanksgiving, let your requests be made known to God;
7 and the peace of God, which surpasses all understanding, will guard your hearts and minds through Christ Jesus.

Joshua 1:8
This Book of the Law shall not depart from your mouth, but you shall meditate in it day and night, that you may observe to do according to all that is written in it. For then you will make your way prosperous, and then you will have good success.

Romans 12:2
And do not be conformed to this world, but be transformed by the renewing of your mind, that you may prove what is that good and acceptable and perfect will of God.

FIND SUCCESS IN YOUR OBEDIENCE

Have you ever thought about what mindset certain people in the Bible must have had, in order to succeed and complete their God-given purpose? Consider the following...

Moses and the Israelites' deliverance out of Egypt (see Exodus 14).
Abraham and his strong belief that God would indeed make his descendants innumerable (see Genesis 26:4).
David's belief that he would one day be king, in spite of Saul's numerous death threats (see 1 Samuel 19).
John the Baptist's humble way of paving the way for Jesus (see Matthew 3).
Jesus' death on the cross (see Matthew 27:32-56).

No doubt, there are countless other examples throughout the Bible that demonstrate a particular, supernatural mindset required to finish what God has ordained. Read Hebrews, chapter eleven, (aka God's Hall of Fame). In the face of trials, tribulations, and obstacles they were able to overcome all and succeed in the purpose in which they were created.

Have you discovered God's purpose for your life but not sure where to start? Have you yet to discover the reason you've been called by God? Well here are a few tools to get you on your way.

Developing a Close Relationship with God.

The more you sit with Him the more you will learn about yourself and about Him (see Luke 10:38-42).

You will begin to know His voice clearly (see John 10:27).

You will begin to see the fenced in things; things you would otherwise never know without God's revelation (see Jeremiah 33:3). Meditate on the Word of God (see Joshua 1:8; 2 Timothy 2:15).

7 BENEFITS of MEDITATING on GOD'S WORD

1. Meditating on God's Word will give you GOOD SUCCESS
2. Meditating on God's Word will make you STRONG and COURAGEOUS
3. Meditating on God's Word will cause you to live a RIGHTEOUS WAY OF LIFE

4. Meditating on God's Word will make you FRUITFUL
5. Meditating on God's Word will give you WISDOM
6. Meditating on God's Word will cause you to SEE JESUS' GLORY

Trust God! Do whatever He tells you to do, go wherever He tells you to go, say whatever He tells you to say and do not be afraid.

Trust that God knows what's best (see Proverbs 3:5).

When He gives you instruction, go with it no matter how illogical it seems (see Proverb 3:6, John 2:5).

God will give you what to say at the right time (see Luke 21:15).

Be Fearless (see 1 Timothy 1:7).

Daily Scripture Reading

Genesis 26:4
And I will make your descendants multiply as the stars of heaven; I will give to your descendants all these lands; and in your seed all the nations of the earth shall be blessed.

John 10:27
My sheep hear My voice, and I know them, and they follow Me.

Jeremiah 33:3
Call to Me, and I will answer you, and show you great and mighty things, which you do not know.

YOU'LL SEE IF YOU BELIEVE

"Jesus said to her, "Did I not say to you that if you would believe you would see the glory of God?" (John 11:40).

I just wanted to encourage you today and let you know that the battle is not yours, but it's the Lord's. It takes a willing heart to release the reigns of your life, all you've believed you were, all the hurt, all the pain, depression, self-doubt, low self-esteem, addiction, not to mention the flesh itself, and place them in the hands of not only another, but someone you've never laid eyes on! But have the faith to believe that He knows what's best for you.

"Do not remember the former things, nor consider the things of old. Behold, I will do a new thing, now it shall spring forth; Shall you not know it? I will even make a road in the wilderness and rivers in the desert" (Isaiah 43:18-19).

Ephesians 3:20 states, *"Now to Him who is able to do exceedingly abundantly above all that we ask or think, according to the power that works in us."*

God is saying that He is the more than we could Ask or Think! This may sound like a cliché, but He really is the Super to your Natural. So no matter how hard the flesh tries, and it will try to fight you, by telling you that nothing will come of this, that your life is fine just the way that it is, that all the pain and hurt you've experienced or bad decisions that you may have made cannot be resolved. But I ask, *"Is anything too hard for the Lord?"* No! He doesn't need much time; He just needs a willing heart. So I say, stand flat-footed against the enemy and declare that the victory belongs to God and Him alone.

And you will see the Glory of God!!!

Daily Scripture Reading

John 11:40
Jesus said to her, "Did I not say to you that if you would believe you would see the glory of God?

Isaiah 43:18-19
Do not remember the former things, nor consider the things of old. Behold, I will do a new thing, now it shall spring forth; Shall you not know it? I will even make a road in the wilderness and rivers in the desert.

JUDGE YOU'RE NOT

"For with what judgment you judge, you will be judged; and with the measure you use, it will be measured back to you" (Matthew 7:2).

Why is it that we're so quick to judge others? Are we naturally conditioned to do so due to our religious backgrounds or home upbringing?

Why is it so easy to find the bad vs. the good in others? Is it due to our own insecurities that keep us from uplifting others?

I personally think that it could be a little of all the above. I also believe that due to us not knowing fully the magnitude of God's love toward us, it's easy for us to believe that God himself couldn't be completely nonjudgmental. Look for yourself. When you do something that you believe is not pleasing to God, you'll look for bad to happen or you'll look not to be blessed. To go a little further, when you see someone do something that you believe is not pleasing to God, you then may have those same feelings towards them. But why should one have those feelings about oneself or about others, when The Word of God clearly states:

"Judge not, that you be not judged. For with what judgment you judge, you will be judged; and with the measure you use, it will be measured back to you" (Matthew 7:1-2).

Which means that the way we judge is the way we can automatically expect to get judged. If we judge harshly or judge at all, then we should not look to receive a lot, if any mercy at all. But guess what? No matter what we do, we'll always look to be granted mercy from others. As Christians it's our duty to restore one who has fallen, not to step on them when they're down.

"Brethren, if a man is overtaken in any trespass, you who are spiritual restore such a one in a spirit of gentleness, considering yourself lest you also be tempted" (Galatians 6:1).

God hasn't given us the authority to judge or condemn others.

"For God did not send His Son into the world to condemn the world, but that the world through Him might be saved" (John 3:17).

Jesus came so that we might have life and that more abundantly! So, allow people to live their life. Allow people to have a personal relationship with the Father that's not based on your biased opinions and assumptions, but that's based purely on getting to know Him and falling in love with Him and allowing Him to do whatever work He wishes to do and complete in each individual.

"When you judge another, you do not define them…you define yourself." — Wayne Dyer

Each and every one of us is a work in and of itself. We have no time to be about other peoples' business. It is truly only by God's grace that we are not consumed. Selah!

Daily Scripture Reading

Matthew 7:1-2
1 Judge not, that you be not judged.
2 For with what judgment you judge, you will be judged; and with the measure you use, it will be measured back to you.

Galatians 6:1
Brethren, if a man is overtaken in any trespass, you who are spiritual restore such a one in a spirit of gentleness, considering yourself lest you also be tempted.

John 3:17
For God did not send His Son into the world to condemn the world, but that the world through Him might be saved.

DRAWING CLOSER TO GOD

Lord, Lead Me in Paths that will Draw Me Closer to You!

"Jesus answered and said to her, 'Martha, Martha, you are worried and troubled about many things. But one thing is needed, and Mary has chosen that good part, which will not be taken away from her'" (Luke 10:41-42).

Drawing closer to God is the single most important thing we could ever do for ourselves. And the enemy knows it.

That's why you may notice when you decide to draw closer to the Creator, distractions from any and everywhere imaginable will come. It can get so bad that you may feel that you were doing better *before* you started to draw closer. But that's the trap that the enemy wants you to fall into. He wants you to give up because boy if you reach the finish line, God wins and he loses!!!

If you pay close attention the battle (distraction) is really never about you. The enemy is not that interested in you. He's just trying to appear better than God. He has always wanted to appear bigger and better. And if he can get you to believe that along the way then that's just a bonus. When drawing closer to God you have to become totally dependent upon Him. If you don't then you will begin to find it harder or maybe even impossible to complete the intended task.

"You will keep him in perfect peace, whose mind is stayed on you, because he trusts in you" (Isaiah 26:3).

You will also need to not only delve into the Word of God but to meditate on it. As you draw closer to God you will begin to become attuned to His voice. Hearing Him through His word will help you to not only stay on the right path, but it will also allow you to understand Him in a whole new way. Prayer will be an essential part of this process. Talking to God through prayer will help the distractions become smaller and smaller. You will feel more centered with the Father and at peace.

"and the peace of God, which surpasses all understanding, will guard your hearts and minds through Christ Jesus" (Philippians 4:7).

Finally, you must trust God as He begins to communicate to you. He knows exactly what's needed to bring you to that expected end (see Jeremiah 29:11). You haven't become who you are today overnight, so trust God as He begins to extract what is not needed from your life in order to infill you with the things that were always fruitful and needful since the beginning of your existence.

He's got your back, You can trust Him!

Daily Scripture Reading

Isaiah 26:3
You will keep him in perfect peace, whose mind is stayed on you, because he trusts in you.

Philippians 4:7
and the peace of God, which surpasses all understanding, will guard your hearts and minds through Christ Jesus.

Jeremiah 29:11
For I know the thoughts that I think toward you, says the Lord, thoughts of peace and not of evil, to give you a future and a hope.

Numbers 23:19
God is not a man, that He should lie, nor a son of man, that He should repent. Has He said, and will He not do? or has He spoken, and will He not make it good?

Luke 10:38-42
38 Now it happened as they went that He entered a certain village; and a certain woman named Martha welcomed Him into her house.
39 And she had a sister called Mary, who also sat at Jesus' feet and heard His word.
40 But Martha was distracted with much serving, and she approached Him and said, "Lord, do You not care that my sister has left me to serve alone? Therefore tell her to help me."
41 And Jesus answered and said to her, "Martha, Martha, you are worried and troubled about many things.
42 But one thing is needed, and Mary has chosen that good part, which will not be taken away from her."

FAITH THAT MOVES

"If you have faith as a mustard seed, you will say to this mountain, 'Move from here to there,' and it will move; and nothing will be impossible for you" (Matthew 17:20).

Whew, have you ever thought about how easy it is to give up? I mean seriously, faith can sometimes be a lot of work. It requires a lot of stamina, energy, strength, and perseverance to see your way through all the darkness. It sometimes makes you want to scream, cry, and shout from the top of your lungs. Having faith and not seeing the results you wish to see may even make you want to blame God or whoever's closest to you. But I've heard that it's in the times of testing that we are made. That's when we find out what we're really made of.

"But He knows the way that I take; When He has tested me, I shall come forth as gold" (Job 23:10).

This morning I woke up to the song *Intentional* by Travis Greene playing in my ear. Intentional means done on purpose; deliberate.

As I started to listen to the song, I really began to think about the word intentional. And It dawned on me that if God allows me to go through something or he allows something to happen then it's not shocking to him. It is intended, designed, conscious, calculated, purposeful and deliberate. He's not vicious, unintentional, thrown off guard, or accidental. He knows exactly what He's doing. He just wants us to trust Him. He wants us to see beyond what is reflected in the mirror of our lives.

I, for one, know that it is not always easy. Here I am having to surrender my worry and doubt to God. I mean at this second. I'm writing and at the same time, I'm trying to let go. I have to let go. He wants me to let go. He needs me to let go.

You have to let go. He wants you to let go. He needs you to let go. He needs us to untie His hands so that He can complete the work He has begun in you.

It's not always pretty. On many occasions and even now, I feel like throwing in the towel. But isn't it something to feel a fight inside of you even when you feel all your strength is gone? That's the amazing part. While I'm here mentally giving up, I mean all actions are pointing to me giving up, yet my spirit is revving up full speed ahead. It won't let me give up. It still wants to hope. It still wants to believe. And for that, I can't seem to flick the off switch on that last glimmer of hope.

"He did not waver at the promise of God through unbelief, but was strengthened in faith, giving glory to God" (Romans 4:21).

Okay, I have to interrupt myself. Did you just see the scripture above? Did you really read and comprehend it?

God promised Abraham who had no children and was at an age that was far beyond seed bearing, that his offspring would be as the stars; innumerable. What did Abraham do? He didn't say no way. He didn't look at his age or his wife's age and say that's impossible. He kept hoping. He believed beyond his natural ability to perceive and he reached into his spiritual capacity to take him to a place in faith that no amount of earthly thoughts could distract God's truth. And for that, His faith was honored.

I'm going to believe because it's not over until God says it's over. Here I am hoping yet again. Believing yet again.

I have to.

Because at the end of the day, I always say that faith is all I have.

Daily Scripture Reading

Matthew 17:20
if you have faith as a mustard seed, you will say to this mountain, 'Move from here to there,' and it will move; and nothing will be impossible for you.

Job 23:10
But He knows the way that I take; When He has tested me, I shall come forth as gold.

Romans 4:18, 20-21
18 who, contrary to hope, in hope believed, so that he became the father of many nations, according to what was spoken, "So shall your descendants be."
20 He did not waver at the promise of God through unbelief, but was strengthened in faith, giving glory to God,
21 and being fully convinced that what He had promised He was also able to perform.

CPSIA information can be obtained
at www.ICGtesting.com
Printed in the USA
BVHW081359071221
623424BV00004B/281